WHAT NOW?

A Teen Guide to Life After High School

Barbara Sheen

ReferencePoint Press®

San Diego, CA

About the Author

Barbara Sheen is the author of 112 books for young people. She lives in New Mexico with her family. In her spare time, she likes to swim, garden, walk, cook, and read.

© 2024 ReferencePoint Press, Inc.
Printed in the United States

For more information, contact:
ReferencePoint Press, Inc.
PO Box 27779
San Diego, CA 92198
www.ReferencePointPress.com

LIBRARY OF CONGRESS CATALOGING-IN-PUBLICATION DATA

Names: Sheen, Barbara, author.
Title: What now? : a teen guide to life after high school / by Barbara
  Sheen.
Description: San Diego, CA : ReferencePoint Press, 2024. | Includes
  bibliographical references and index.
Identifiers: LCCN 2023002514 (print) | LCCN 2023002515 (ebook) | ISBN
  9781678206000 (library binding) | ISBN 9781678206017 (ebook)
Subjects: LCSH: Self-help techniques for teenagers--Juvenile literature. |
  Self-confidence in adolescence--Juvenile literature. | Vocational
  guidance--Juvenile literature.
Classification: LCC BF632 .S514 2024 (print) | LCC BF632 (ebook) | DDC
  158.10835--dc23
LC record available at https://lccn.loc.gov/2023002514
LC ebook record available at https://lccn.loc.gov/2023002515

Contents

At a Crossroads

When Jessica graduated from high school, she was unprepared for the future. Most of her classmates were headed to college, but Jessica was tired of sitting in a classroom. Unaware of other options, she decided to go right into the workforce. Without any idea about what she wanted to do, she wound up bouncing from one low-paying clerical job to another. None of these positions suited her high-energy personality, and she was barely earning enough money to get by. "I tried doing office work," she recalls. "But it was very tedious. I hated sitting still all day. I'm more of a hands-on person."[1]

After three years of feeling at sea, she heard about a trainee position at a local pest control company. Although she had never considered a career in pest control, she decided to give it a shot. She says, "This was a trade I could learn. It's in demand. Once I get licensed, I can make good money, and I like this work. I'm moving around, and I meet lots of people. It's just too bad I didn't know about this type of training program sooner."[2]

An Important Time

It took Jessica three years to find her path, and she is not alone. Graduating from high school marks a crossroads in a person's life. It is a time to celebrate personal achievement as well as a time when young people transition from the restraints of childhood to adulthood.

High school graduates who are eighteen or older are considered adults. As adults, they have more freedom and control over their lives but also more responsibilities. Up until this point, most young people's lives have been controlled by their parents and their school schedule. They were unlikely to have much input into where they lived, what they studied in school, how they managed their time, or how they earned or spent money. But once they graduate high school, they are expected to start taking care of themselves and making their own decisions. Zakirah White, a recent high school graduate, explains:

> "My life after high school has been many things; change, growth, maturity, a lot of anxiety, learning, unlearning and joy. . . . Having so much power over your own life all at once can be very overwhelming at first."[3]
>
> —Zakirah White, high school graduate

> My life after high school has been many things; change, growth, maturity, a lot of anxiety, learning, unlearning and joy. . . .
>
> Having so much power over your own life all at once can be very overwhelming at first. After moving across the country to California and saying goodbye to the comfort of my parent's home, I found that with this newfound freedom I was also now responsible for things like my health, bills, whether or not I was eating properly, time management, money management, even things that I thought were supposed to happen naturally like my personal happiness.
>
> At first, every decision I made on this journey felt like it held so much weight because of the many outcomes that could take place. I would constantly question myself.[3]

Graduating from high school marks a crossroads in life. It is a time of transition from childhood to adulthood.

What's Next?

Indeed, life after high school is a time for decision-making. High school graduates are expected to make big decisions about their future that have a major impact on their lives. The biggest—and often the scariest—decision high school graduates must make is what to do next. There are lots of paths a high school graduate can follow. They may decide to continue their education. If so, they must determine what they want to study and where as well as whether this will be in a four-year or two-year college or in a vocational or technical training school. Alternatively, they may decide to enter the workforce, and then they must decide on the type of work they want to do. Or they may opt to join the military or start their own business. Some choose to take a year off to travel, volunteer, learn a new skill, or pursue a passion, among other activities.

Selecting the right path is personal. It often depends on a person's career goals since different careers require distinct levels of training and education. Some teens know exactly what they want to do with their lives. Many others do not. In fact, it is normal to be uncertain about the future, especially when there are so many decisions to be made and these decisions hold a high degree of consequence. However, no decision is irrevocable, a fact that can help ease the stress of the decision-making process. Even those individuals who seem to know exactly what they want frequently wind up veering onto a different path.

Over time, people grow and change, as do their interests, plans, and goals. Students often change their field of study, and workers shift their career fields. In fact, according to the US Department of Education, a third of all college students change their majors at least once, and the Bureau of Labor Statistics (BLS) reports that average workers have twelve jobs during their work lives.

Moving Ahead

Clearly, transitioning from childhood to adulthood is a daunting task, and making decisions about what to do after high school can be overwhelming. Knowing that decisions can be changed might help ease stress. And thinking about the future and learning more about the various options that are available can help teens move forward with confidence while enjoying the journey.

Chapter One

Preparing and Exploring

Matt is a young man who was undecided about what to do after high school. Everyone expected him to go right to college, but the prospect did not excite him. He preferred working with his hands to traditional academics. Nonetheless, he enrolled in college. Although he did well in his classes, after one semester, he knew he was on the wrong path.

Dissatisfied with his life, he started thinking about what he really wanted to do, what he was good at, and what made him happy. He realized that he did not want to spend the next four years in a traditional classroom; he wanted to do something else, something in sync with his strengths and interests. He enjoyed problem solving and fixing things, was manually dexterous, physically fit, and fascinated by electronics. So, he started investigating careers that would utilize his skills and interests but did not require a college degree.

Bucking pressure from his family, at the end of his freshman year he dropped out of college and took a job as an electrician's helper. In this position, he collaborated with an experienced electrician who taught him everything he needed to learn to become a licensed electrician. It was not the path others might have planned for him, but it suited him. He explains, "Sometimes you feel that society says you have to go to college, especially if you're a good student, and I went through that battle in my head. But I knew I had to figure out what was right for me. And now that I have, I don't regret my choice at all."[4]

A Personal Decision

Like Matt, many young people are unsure about what they want to do after high school. Some enter the workforce without thinking about what type of work suits them. They take the first job they are offered even though it does not interest them. Or they enter a family business that bores them because that is what is expected of them.

Without considering their own dreams, others enroll in college because their parents pressure them to do so. Many also choose a college major based on what their parents want, even if the major is not right for them. That is what Jenny Mills did. Mills, the founder and director of the social welfare organization Limitless Child International, recalls,

> It took me three years of college in a pre-nursing program before I realized I had absolutely no desire to be a nurse. None. My parents really wanted me to be a nurse and there were a lot of expectations put on me. . . . I had no drive for academics. What I did have was a passion for the idea of travel and I dreamt that someday I would have a job that would take me all over the world, but at that time it was like wishing I had a job that would take me to the moon. It wasn't possible. What was possible was a good job in nursing. So I ignored my true heart's leaning and dutifully applied and got into the local university. My junior year we started our clinical rotations, and I couldn't bear it anymore.

I was miserable. I took some time off, returned briefly to get a degree in biology, and found myself at the library studying maps of India and China instead of physiology. Finally, it dawned on me that what I really wanted to do was social work, preferably in a foreign country. Once that clicked, my path was clear—at least to me. My parents took some convincing. It took me several years and lots of grief to figure out what I really wanted to do, but it was totally worth it.[5]

Indeed, although the opinions of family and friends can be helpful, every person's path is unique. Planning the future based on others' expectations can lead to problems, yet that is exactly what many young people do.

Looking Inward

Taking time to get to know themselves better can help teens avoid these pitfalls. As writer and entrepreneur Eric S. Burdon, explains, "To learn about yourself is to provide yourself direction and depth. . . . It's the start of a desire to take control of your life. . . . In times where so many of us are unsure of who we are and where we want to be, to take time to learn about yourself is crucial."[6]

One of the best ways teens can better understand what they want to do with their lives is to look inward. Thinking about their accomplishments, strengths and weaknesses, interests, personal values, dreams, and goals is a good place to start. To help guide them, teens should consider which school subjects are their favorites, what they like to do in their free time, what they do or do not do well, what they believe to be most important in life, whether they prefer group or solo activities, whether they enjoy moving around or sitting still, and whether they tend to lead or follow.

"In times where so many of us are unsure of who we are and where we want to be, to take time to learn about yourself is crucial."[6]

—Eric S. Burdon, writer and entrepreneur

Many careers do not require a college degree for entry. A beginning electrician, for example, can start straight out of high school and learn on the job from an experienced mentor.

In addition, they can take a self-assessment quiz to better understand who they are. These quizzes ask test takers questions about their values, personality traits, likes and dislikes, and work style. There are no right or wrong answers, and most of these tests are fun to take. They are available in books, online, and often through school counselors. Most are free. The US Department of Labor's CareerOneStop website offers three free self-assessment tests. The Occupational Information Network (O*NET), an online job database sponsored by the US government, also offers a comprehensive interest profiler test.

Investigating Careers

Upon completing the quiz, test takers receive an assessment of their interests and personality and, usually, a list of careers and career fields that are aligned with their interests and temperament. Although the results of these tests are not definitive, they do help teens learn more about themselves, which can help them narrow down their choices.

Dominant Personality Types

Many self-assessment tests group people into six dominant personality types: realistic, investigative, artistic, social, enterprising, and conventional. These classifications are used to match people with occupations that sync with their personality type.

Here are some of the characteristics of each personality type:

- Realistic personalities prefer hands-on activities, working with plants, animals, tools, and machines. They see themselves as practical and mechanical.
- Investigative types like solving math and science problems. They see themselves as scientific.
- Artistic personalities enjoy art, writing, dance, music, drama, crafts, and other artistic pursuits. They view themselves as expressive and creative.
- Social personalities like to help others and solve social problems. They are generally good at teaching, caregiving, counseling, and giving information. They see themselves as helpful and friendly.
- Enterprising personalities are leaders and communicators. They are good at selling things and ideas. They are often interested in business and politics and view themselves as sociable and ambitious.
- Conventional personalities are orderly. They like structure and enjoy working with numbers and written records. They consider themselves good at following a plan and value success in business.

Using what they have learned, young people can start researching career fields and specific occupations that align with their aptitudes, interests, goals, and values while eliminating those that do not mesh with their unique personality. For instance, someone who is interested in investigating and solving crimes; prefers working in a quiet, indoor environment; and does not enjoy lots of social interaction might be happier working as a cybersecurity analyst than as a police officer. Although individuals in both professions share similar goals and interests, some important aspects of a police officer's work conflict with this person's personality.

Teens can further narrow their investigation by considering the potential earnings and future job outlook for occupations that interest them. Some career fields face shortages of qualified workers. Skilled workers in high-demand fields have a high earning potential. Moreover, employment opportunities in most of these fields are predicted to continue to grow. As a result, potential employees face less competition to get hired and have some assurance that they will be needed in the future.

Knowing the educational requirements of a career is also important. For example, it can take eleven years or more beyond high school to become a physician. Therefore, individuals who are interested in a career in health care but do not want to commit to the extensive education and training necessary to become a physician should consider other careers in health care, such as a nurse, physician's assistant, diagnostic medical sonographer, or respiratory therapist, positions that do not require as much education and training.

Self-assessment quizzes gather information about a person's likes, values, work style, and other qualities and compile a list of possible career matches.

Helpful Options

There are several ways teens can learn about different careers. The BLS, for example, publishes an online *Occupational Outlook Handbook*, which gives information about approximately eight hundred occupations. This information includes data on what each job entails, the skills and personality traits each position requires, working conditions, salary, future employment projections, and the education and training that each job requires.

The handbook also divides occupations among twenty-five career fields, such as arts and design, business and financial, health care, military, and sales. Clicking on a career field provides teens with a list of, and information about, a variety of occupations in that field. By utilizing this feature, teens who know they are interested in a certain occupational field can simplify their research. For more detailed information, the BLS provides an online *Career Outlook* publication that features interviews with workers in a wide range of careers. In addition, it offers materials to students, including a career exploration section that allows individuals to explore different career paths based on their interests.

Young people can also learn more about careers that interest them in other ways. Many schools host career days in which

Financial Preparation

As teens prepare for the future, they should not ignore financial issues. Life after high school can be costly. Postsecondary education is expensive. Even if young people opt to go directly into the job market, their starting salary may be small. Nevertheless, they need money to pay for transportation, food, and rent. Those with a car must pay for car insurance, gas, and maintenance. And those who decide to take some time off before pursuing postsecondary education or entering the job market will need funds to pay for gap year activities such as travel.

Consequently, saving money is important. Opening an interest-bearing savings account and making regular deposits is a good starting point. Experts recommend people save a set amount each week. Even if the amount is small, over time it adds up. Plus, the interest a savings account earns increases the balance. Conserving some money is also a great practice that will help build an individual's financial stability into adulthood.

community members in various careers give presentations and answer questions about their jobs. Some schools also invite representatives from different colleges and vocational schools to participate. These representatives present information about the role postsecondary education plays in achieving career goals. In addition, some high schools offer a career planning elective class that introduces students to a wide range of careers.

Volunteering, doing service activities, and working in fields that interest them is another way teens can explore potential careers. Tutoring younger students, volunteering in an after-school program, or working as a summer camp counselor, for example, are all effective ways for individuals interested in a career in education to see whether working with children is a good match for their skills and personality while getting hands-on experience in the field. Job shadowing, which involves following and observing a professional through a typical workday, is still another way for young people to learn more about different jobs and whether an occupation is right for them. As an article on the employment website Indeed states,

> "Job shadowing for high school students is important because it can help you understand different jobs and careers before entering the workforce. Exploring potential careers to pursue can also help you decide whether you want to enroll in a degree program or trade school after high school."[7]
>
> —Indeed Editorial Team

Job shadowing for high school students is important because it can help you understand different jobs and careers before entering the workforce. Exploring potential careers to pursue can also help you decide whether you want to enroll in a degree program or trade school after high school. For example, if you shadowed an account manager as they performed their daily routines, you might decide to pursue an education in accounting and a career in account management.[7]

Starting Early

Once teens have a specific or even general idea about what they want to do, they can start preparing long before they graduate. Taking college preparatory classes, for example, is vital if their career choice requires a college degree. So is getting good grades, which will help them get into the college of their choice and possibly secure a scholarship. Choosing classes related to their field of interest is also helpful. Someone who is interested in becoming an architect, for instance, can start preparing for this career by taking classes in art, mathematics, and computer science, all of which develop skills that are essential in this profession. Doing so also prepares potential architects for higher-level college courses that are part of this college major.

Similarly, getting involved in extracurricular activities related to their field of interest or college major is another way to sharpen

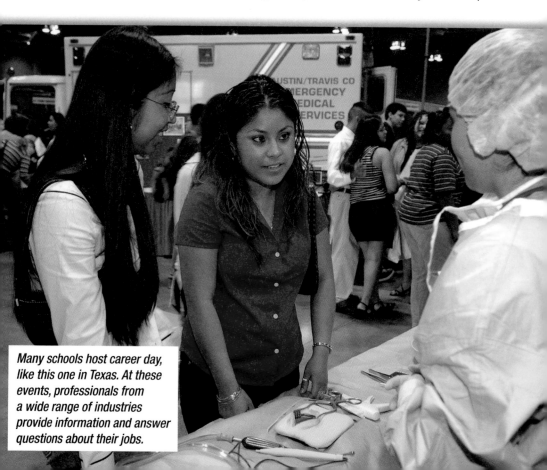

Many schools host career day, like this one in Texas. At these events, professionals from a wide range of industries provide information and answer questions about their jobs.

skills vital for success in various career fields. Future event planners might consider joining a prom planning committee, whereas potential politicians, diplomats, and community organizers might take on a role in student government, join a debate club, or participate in Model United Nations activities. And those interested in a career in social or traditional media might choose to work on school publications, anchor school video newscasts, or participate in photography and film clubs. Indeed, even participating in extracurricular activities that are unrelated to a particular occupation or college major can be useful. Many activities, such as being a member of a sports team or participating in band or school theater, help teens develop leadership and interpersonal skills that are applicable to almost all professions.

There are many steps teens can take to help them determine what they want to do after high school. Learning about themselves, investigating careers, and starting to prepare as early as possible can help them reach their goals.

Chapter Two

Going to College

Megan is a student at Columbia University who hopes to someday become a lawyer. Even before her senior year in high school, Megan knew that she wanted to go to a prestigious college and then an equally respected law school. Her plans influenced her decision to go to college and her choice of an Ivy League school. As she explains,

Education has always been a strong part of my life. I've always been a good student. It was one of my defining traits. . . . I became interested in law after taking some electives in high school. . . . I want to go to law school, that's my formal education, end goal. . . . I was really conscious of this when I was applying [to colleges]. I want to go to a law school that's prestigious and rigorous, so I need to attend a similar undergraduate university. The top law schools definitely consider your undergraduate degree. I want to get a foot in the door with more competitive graduate schools. . . . Columbia opens doors.[8]

The Benefits of Going to College

Like Megan, more than 60 percent of American high school graduates enroll in college immediately after high school, according to the National Center for Education Statistics (NCES). Forty-three percent enroll in a four-year college, and 20 percent enroll in a two-year college.

There are many reasons why getting a college education is so popular. A bachelor's or associate's degree is required for approximately one-third of all jobs in the United States, according to Pearson Education, an educational publishing company. Even when a college degree is not required, employers are often more likely to prefer a job candidate with a degree. Therefore, having a college degree expands the number and types of jobs that candidates qualify for and makes it easier for them to find suitable work.

It is possible for individuals to earn a comfortable living without a postsecondary education, but having a college degree increases a person's earning potential. According to the BLS, people with a bachelor's degree earn an average of $64,896 per year, and those with an associate's degree averaged $46,124 annually. In comparison, individuals with just a high school diploma earn an average of $38,792.

Going to college offers other benefits too. It provides students with the opportunity to meet and get to know people from diverse backgrounds. It also exposes them to different viewpoints and gives them the chance to explore new interests, all of which enhance their personal growth. As college student Zakirah White explains, "This new stage of life causes a lot of things to be put into perspective, forces you to question the beliefs you always held about the world as a child, pushes you to form your own views and opinions . . . and allows you to meet so many people from so many backgrounds and cultures."[9]

In college, students are exposed to people of diverse backgrounds and viewpoints. This type of exposure can lead to personal growth.

Associate's or Bachelor's Degree?

Teens who decide to pursue a college education must decide whether they want to go for an associate's or a bachelor's degree. It usually takes two years of full-time study, or about 60 credit hours, to earn an associate's degree. In comparison, students must complete about 120 credit hours to earn a bachelor's degree, which generally takes four years of full-time study.

There are different types of associate's degrees. An associate of science, applied science, or applied arts degree prepares students for specific careers. In contrast, an associate of arts degree focuses on liberal arts studies; often, the coursework may be transferred toward a bachelor's degree in the future. Most students earn an associate's degree at a community college. Community colleges are public institutions. Many offer open enrollment to anyone with a high school diploma or a general equivalency diploma. Community colleges differ from four-year schools in significant ways. Only a few community colleges have on-campus housing. Most students live at home and commute. Some are raising families and working while taking classes. To better serve a diverse student body, most community colleges offer flexible scheduling options and online classes.

Some students choose to attend a community college to save money. In fact, nearly thirty states offer tuition-free community college to students who meet specific criteria, which differ from state to state. However, the difference in future earnings potential between associate's and bachelor's degree holders helps offset the higher cost of earning a bachelor's degree.

Choosing a Four-Year College

Four-year colleges offer a more traditional college experience. There are hundreds of schools to choose from and many things to consider, including a school's size and location, whether it is public or private, and the available fields of study. The school's reputation, campus life, the cost, and an individual's chances of acceptance

Handling the Stress of Applying to College

Applying to college is stressful. Among other things, students worry about what schools to apply to, whether their dream school will accept them, and whether they will be offered sufficient financial aid. College counselor Lindsey Conger, offers teens the following tips to help them cope with the pressure:

> Start early by visiting admission websites, talking to college students or representatives, and attending information sessions to figure out where you might want to attend college. The Common Application prompts are released before summer even starts, so you could get started on your personal statement as soon as possible. . . .

> Luckily, the Common App makes it easier for students to apply to multiple schools a little quicker. You won't have to fill out your basic information numerous times, and you can send your personal statement to all the universities that accept the Common App. . . . As you apply to more schools, you might realize you have to write about a similar topic for multiple schools. Reuse the content when you can, but make sure that each essay is still tailored to the particular school and fully answers the specific prompt.

Lindsey Conger, "5 Ways to Manage College Application Stress Effectively," CollegeXpress, November 11, 2021. www.collegexpress.com.

are other important considerations. It is typically less expensive, for example, to attend public colleges than private institutions. Data from a 2022 *U.S. News & World Report* survey found that the average cost of tuition and fees at an in-state four-year public college is about 72 percent less than for a private college. Public colleges are sometimes larger than private colleges. They may also offer more fields of study and more diverse campus activities.

Class size also varies significantly. The student-faculty ratio in large public institutions is usually greater than in smaller schools. Students attending large schools are less likely to get to know their instructors well or to receive one-on-one instruction. Moreover, many private colleges strive to foster mentoring relationships between professors and students. Zack, a student at Amherst College, admits that class size was one of the main reasons he chose the small private school. He says, "I knew that smaller classrooms and the ability to meet and form relationships with my professors were a high priority. Also, admittedly, not having the longest attention span, I knew a large lecture hall class would set me up for failure."[10]

Where a college is located is another deciding factor. Rural and urban colleges have different atmospheres and offer students different recreational opportunities. Students attending an urban college can take advantage of all the resources cities have to offer, whereas the availability of outdoor activities attracts many young people to rural schools. Jake, a student at Dartmouth College, prefers the outdoor experience. "I couldn't imagine being somewhere I couldn't be active," he says. "Skiing, hiking, swimming and other hobbies would be very difficult if not impossible in a city environment. While not always the case, the more rural schools I looked at offered much more than a college campus but a lifestyle as well."[11]

> "I knew that smaller classrooms [at a private college] and the ability to meet and form relationships with my professors were a high priority. Also, admittedly, not having the longest attention span, I knew a large lecture hall class would set me up for failure."[10]
>
> —Zack, Amherst College student

Small class size, where students can experience one-on-one interaction with the instructor, is a major draw for some prospective students.

Distance from home is important too. Some young adults are comfortable attending a college far from home. In fact, many teens want the experience of living in a place that is different, environmentally and culturally, from their hometown. Others, such as Annie, a recent University of Tennessee graduate, opt to remain closer to home. "I went to University of Tennessee, Knoxville," she explains. "I chose that school because it was a few hours' drive from home, far enough away to be independent, yet close enough to drive. I loved being able to see my family whenever I wanted."[12]

Considering such factors can help students narrow down their potential college choices. They can find more information about these colleges—and hundreds more—on the College Navigator, a free online tool sponsored by the NCES. This resource provides details about tuition costs, programs and majors, campus security, and other data to help college-bound students make informed decisions. Guidebooks, college websites, and school guidance counselors are other useful sources of information; so are college fairs, which many high schools sponsor. Touring college campuses, and talking to students, professors, and financial aid officers, either in person or virtually, also helps in the decision-making process. Louise Lyall, a University of Wisconsin–Madison student, explains how she narrowed down her choices: "If I heard about a college that sounded interesting, I went through a big college guidebook and read about it. Then, if it still looked good to me I went online and checked out the website and looked it up on Wikipedia. If the school still interested me . . . I googled pictures of the campus. If, after all that, I still liked the school I put it on my list."[13]

The Application Process

Once teens have narrowed down their choices, they can begin the application process. Most college application deadlines fall between November and March of students' senior year in high school. A typical four-year college application is composed of many elements and can take weeks to complete. To save time, students can apply to multiple schools using the same application. Known as the Common Application, it is accepted by over one thousand colleges. Applicants must include information about their awards, achievements, and extracurricular activities. They will also be asked to append a copy of their high school transcripts, letters of recommendation, financial information, and an essay. Some schools also require students to participate in an interview with an admissions officer. Students who plan to major in subjects such as art and design or filmmaking may also be required to submit a portfolio of their work.

In the past, standardized test scores were also required. However, according to a survey sponsored by Kaplan, an educational services corporation, only 5 percent of colleges surveyed required standardized test scores for the 2021–2022 school year. Applicants can check a school's website to find out whether standardized test scores are required as well as whether the school accepts the Common Application.

Experts recommend that students apply to between five and eight schools. These, they advise, should include one to three reach schools, three to five match schools, and one or two safety schools. College admission officers use these terms to describe the likelihood of whether students will be accepted at a particular college. Reach schools are typically schools that have extremely high educational standards and low admission rates. However, any college can be considered a reach school if an applicant's grade point average (GPA) is below that of the average admitted student. Although gaining entry to a reach school is a long shot, in some instances an applicant's talents, background, essay, and letters of recommendation will take precedence over academic performance.

The odds of students getting into their match schools are better but not guaranteed. Match schools are schools in which an applicant's GPA equals that of the average admitted first-year

Loan-Free Need-Based Financial Aid

Because so many students graduate from college in debt, approximately seventy-two US colleges have adopted no-loan financial aid policies. Instead of offering students who qualify for need-based financial aid loans that must be paid back, these schools offer loan-free financial assistance. According to Kevin Ladd, chief operating officer and creator of Scholarships.com, "No-loan schools are basically telling students of modest or even extremely low income that they should apply if they have the grades and extracurricular (activities) to be considered, and that they do not have to worry about the high price tag as long as they are able to get accepted." Princeton University, Williams College (Massachusetts), the University of Florida, and the College of the Ozarks (Missouri) are just a few of these schools. Each school differs in the income level that families must fall below to qualify for loan-free financial aid. For example, starting in the fall of 2023, Princeton will offer students whose families earn less than $100,000 a year full-ride scholarships covering all college expenses. Likewise, Haverford College (Pennsylvania) limits its loan-free program to students whose families earn less than $60,000 a year.

Quoted in Sarah Wood and Cole Claybourne, "No Loan Colleges: What to Know," *U.S. News & World Report*, September 22, 2022. www.usnews.com.

student. Students have the best chance of being accepted into their safety schools. These are schools in which an applicant's GPA exceeds that of the average freshman.

Paying for College

Most colleges charge a $50 application fee. But application fees are just the beginning. Tuition and fees can reach more than $74,000 a year at some institutions. In addition, students must pay for their textbooks and supplies, which cost about $1,200 a year, according to the College Board, a company that designs standardized tests. Room and board are also costly, averaging about $11,000 a year, according to the NCES. Therefore, it is not surprising that *Forbes* reports that more than half of all college students leave school owing an average of $28,950. Nevertheless, there are a variety of steps teens can take to offset the cost of college, such as attending an in-state public college, starting out at a community college, and applying early for financial aid.

Many organizations award scholarships to students who face financial, cultural, health, or learning challenges. School counselors can help teens find out about these options.

Financial aid comes in the form of scholarships, grants, loans, and work-study programs. Experts advise potential college students to complete the Free Application for Federal Student Aid (FAFSA). Colleges use FAFSA data to establish whether students are eligible for federal financial aid. According to the NCES, approximately 87 percent of full-time college students receive some type of federal financial aid.

In addition to federal financial aid, almost every college awards academic and athletic scholarships to outstanding candidates. Plus, many organizations award scholarships to students who face financial, cultural, health, or learning challenges. Members of different clubs and ethnic groups, as well as the children of parents who work in a particular field or business, are also candidates for aid. School counselors can help teens find out about these options, and there are several online scholarship databases that students can search. In addition, many private colleges offer generous financial aid packages to students who cannot afford tuition.

> "There is a magic that happens in a college classroom and on a college campus that cannot be reproduced anywhere, and for this reason alone, it is worth considering as an option."[14]
>
> —Genevieve Morgan, author

Undoubtedly, choosing to go to college right after high school is a big decision. There is a lot to consider. Nonetheless, many individuals say that opting to go to college was one of the best decisions they ever made. As Genevieve Morgan, author of *Undecided: Navigating Life and Learning After High School,* explains, "There is a magic that happens in a college classroom and on a college campus that cannot be reproduced anywhere, and for this reason alone, it is worth considering as an option."[14]

Chapter Three

Opting for Technical and Vocational Training

When Charlie Tran graduated from high school, he was undecided about what he wanted to do next. He was mechanically minded and dreamed of traveling. But with no career plan in mind and few marketable skills, he took a job as a server in a restaurant. When the business shut down, he was unemployed. Looking for work, he clicked on a link from a career website that described the fastest-growing jobs in the United States. He explains:

> The first thing that popped up was wind turbine technician. Growing up in the South, I had never seen a wind turbine, but I thought to myself, "That it would be a really cool career!" When I researched more about this career, it drew me closer to picking it. It matched everything I had always liked doing—being outdoors, seeing new places and maintaining things.

I then researched some schools and decided to choose Kalamazoo Valley Community College because they offered the fast-track, six-month Wind Turbine Technician Academy (WTTA), which is a highly sought-after and hands-on accredited program. After completion of WTTA, I landed my traveling job maintaining turbines. I would have never thought I could see different parts of the U.S. while getting paid.[15]

What Are Technical and Vocational Programs?

Tran trained for his job through a vocational training program at a community college. Besides offering traditional academic courses, community colleges offer programs that award diplomas, certificates, and associate's degrees in science, applied arts, or applied science in a wide range of vocational and technical fields. Vocational and technical institutes offer similar programs.

Four-year college is not right for everyone. Individuals like Tran, who prefer hands-on activities to traditional academics, as well as those who want a shorter path to a well-paying, in-demand career, often thrive in a technical or vocational training program that prepares them for a specific occupation. These individuals are no less intelligent than their peers who opt to pursue a bachelor's degree; they just have different interests and learning styles.

Technical and vocational training programs, which are also known as career and technical education programs, aim to get participants out of the classroom and into a job in their chosen field quickly. The coursework focuses on specific fields of study rather than liberal arts, and it commonly involves lots of laboratory and field experience. Students learn through practice under the supervision of instructors who are experienced professionals in the field of study. For example, students training to become welders spend most of their time learning to use a variety of welding tools safely and effectively. They hone their skills by completing a variety of welding projects. Much of what they learn is designed to prepare them for obtaining certification with the American Welding Society.

The time to complete a vocational and technical training program can range from a few weeks of intensive preparation to a two-year commitment in an associate's degree program, depending on the field of study and the school. Most programs offer flexible scheduling, online classes, multiple start dates, and financial aid packages. They also assist graduates in securing suitable employment. In fact, many businesses partner with schools to ensure that the instruction given to students aligns with their companies' needs. For instance, to obtain qualified workers to fill current and future positions, Pacific Gas and Electric (PG&E) partners with several community colleges in California. As part of this partnership, PG&E provides the schools with technical support, a specially designed curriculum, instructors who are industry experts, and training equipment. As Walter Bumphus, president of the American Association of Community Colleges, states,

Vocational and technical training programs teach students the skills they need to perform very specific jobs, such as wind turbine technician.

"As colleges reimagine their roles for the 21st century, they are committing to work with businesses and industry to provide trained and adaptable talent. We encourage companies to work with their community college partners to develop programs and pipelines that meet their current and future needs."[16]

Opportunities in Many Fields

Students who opt for vocational and technical training can choose from a wide range of career fields. They can prepare for careers in aerospace, computer science, construction, health care, mechanical science, and other technical fields. Many of these fields have more job openings than qualified applicants and offer generous salaries and benefits. Young people interested in building and construction, for example, can train to be plumbers, electricians, building inspectors, or heating, ventilating, and air-conditioning (HVAC) technicians, just to name a few possibilities. These are in-demand occupations that provide skilled professionals with a good income. For example, according to Payscale, as of February 2022, HVAC technicians earned an average of $63,264 annually. Joe Strada, an HVAC professional, remarks, "I think what's surprising about our profession is the amount of money people can make, and how well they could support their family. This is a great industry that's always in demand. You need . . . to be comfortable and cool. And those are two really important things that people won't go without."[17]

Qualified health care workers are also highly sought-after. Research suggests that the demand for health care workers will outpace the supply by 2025. Community colleges and vocational institutes prepare interested individuals to become licensed medical and dental assistants, respiratory therapists, phlebotomists, medical sonographers, additional medical imaging technicians,

The Benefits of Vocational and Technical Training

Opting to get vocational and technical training has many benefits. The training costs less and takes less time to complete than a bachelor's degree program, and graduates can expect to earn more than individuals who just hold a high school diploma.

Small classes and individualized instruction, hands-on training, and career placement services are other benefits. According to the Imagine America Foundation (IAF), an organization that supports postsecondary career education training programs, "Many institutions have counselors whose only job is to find their students employment once they earn their certificate or degree. This shows how dedicated schools are to your success. It also helps them provide targeted hands-on training, internships, and industry-specific training so that you can be successful both in the classroom and on the job."

In addition, these programs keep up with new industry trends and technology. The IAF states, "This means that you'll get an up-to-date degree [or certificate] that prepares you to be ready on day one of your new job. Having a relevant skill set will make you more marketable and desirable to employers and the clients you will one day work with."

Imagine America Foundation, "The 8 Benefits of Going to a Trade School," March 8, 2019. www.imagine-america.org.

and other rewarding health care careers. For these careers, students take classes in biology and anatomy as well as classes that concentrate on practical skills related to the field of study. For instance, the coursework for medical sonographers focuses on operating ultrasound and imaging equipment. Students practice by scanning one another. They also scan actual patients under the supervision of an experienced sonographer. As part of their training, students in almost all health care specialties rotate through hospitals or other medical facilities to get real-world experience.

Other programs prepare technology-minded young people for careers in information technology (IT). Jobs in this industry are predicted to grow by double digits in the next ten years. Depending on the school and program, students can earn an associate's degree in information technology and computer science or certification in cloud computing, cybersecurity fundamentals, computer programming, or web design, to name a few choices. Trésor Mwali is a young man who earned an associate of applied science degree in IT from the Community College of Vermont. Before earning the degree, he was working as a housekeeper. His dislike of that job motivated him to go back to school to pursue a career in his passion: computer science. After completing the IT program, Mwali landed a good job as a technical support specialist at a bank. "Today I have a better life," he says. "I love what I'm doing. I love computer stuff, I'm working with them and it's really amazing for me."[18]

Qualified health care workers, such as this phlebotomist, are in high demand. Vocational and technical training programs prepare students for careers in this area.

Specialty Programs for Creative Individuals

Not everyone who opts for vocational training is interested in a technical career. Vocational programs also offer training in fields that let students showcase their creative side. These fields include, but are not limited to, art and design, fashion, culinary arts, cosmetology, and creative media technology. As a case in point, individuals who love working with others, are interested in the beauty industry, and who enjoy styling hair, applying makeup, practicing nail art, and caring for skin often flourish in cosmetology programs. These programs combine practical training in which students work on real people in a salon-like setting with business classes that prepare potential beauty professionals to own and manage their own businesses in the future. Usually, with no more than one year of training, students can become licensed cosmetology professionals.

Graduates are employed as hairstylists, barbers, estheticians, makeup artists, and nail techs. With experience, they can move into such positions as salon and spa owners, cosmetology instructors, and beauty product sales professionals. Indeed, many cosmetologists do multiple things. As Atlanta salon owner and award-winning hairstylist Daniel Holzberger explains, "I've done hair shows . . . I've worked behind the chair, I've owned salons, I've owned barber shops, I own a scissor company. . . . If you go into cosmetology your options are limitless, they really are."[19]

According to the BLS, job openings in the beauty industry are growing faster than the average rate. Moreover, industry professionals can earn a comfortable income. ZipRecruiter, an employment marketplace for job seekers, reports that average income ranges from about $35,000 to $70,000. However, these figures do not include tips, which usually make up a big portion of a cosmetologist's yearly income.

"If you go into cosmetology your options are limitless, they really are."[19]

—Daniel Holzberger, award-winning hairstylist

Culinary Arts Programs

Individuals who express their artistic talent through cooking can train in culinary arts at a community college or culinary institute. Potential bakers and chefs work in state-of-the-art laboratories under the supervision of experts. The coursework generally includes, but is not limited to, instruction in food safety, nutrition, menu planning, and different kitchen operations. Laboratory classes focus on specific careers. For instance, future chefs practice different cooking styles, and potential bakers and pastry chefs practice working with bread dough, cake decorating, and pastry art. Students sample and critique each other's dishes and take part in competitions and catering events. In many programs, students participate in unpaid work-study experiences before graduating, working beside industry professionals and testing their skills in restaurant and hotel kitchens. Plus, they make industry connections that can help them once they begin their careers.

Teens who pursue culinary arts training should be aware that starting salaries in the industry are low and the competition for good jobs is stiff. Nevertheless, culinary arts training helps individuals who love working with food get their foot in the door, and, over time, become leaders in the industry.

Other creative individuals might consider enrolling in creative media technology programs. These prepare students for careers in video game design, computer animation, and digital video, film, and graphics. Young artists who love gaming and computers, for instance, can earn an associate's degree or certification in video game design. Video game designers are responsible for creating the concepts, characters, stories, and visual designs that make up video games. Since games are created using lines of computer code, the coursework includes instruction in programming and coding related to gaming technology. Students also learn and practice digital editing, 3-D modeling, and animation. Working in teams, they use their skills and talents to create and build actual games, which they test out by playing the game with other team members.

The video game industry is a very hot and growing field. Payscale reports that certified game designers earn between $40,000 and $104,000 a year. The average salary is about $67,000. For creative people, it is just one of many fields that they can train for at a community college or vocational institution.

Selecting a School

Hands-on programs such as these are offered at community colleges and private institutions. However, many experts advise students to choose a community college program whenever possible. Most private vocational and technical schools are for-profit businesses and are usually considerably more expensive than community colleges. In fact, it is not unheard-of for tuition and fees at these schools to be as much as ten times that charged by community colleges for a similar course of study.

Community colleges are also more reliable. Although most for-profit technical and vocational schools are trustworthy, a few have been found guilty of unethical practices. Some schools have declared bankruptcy and shut down overnight. In many of these

Creative students may flourish in careers such as hairdressing, which provide steady work and income along with an artistic outlet.

cases, students were not given tuition refunds. Some students lost their financial aid, and many were left with worthless credits that were not accepted by other educational facilities.

To avoid such pitfalls, before applying to a for-profit private institution, students can take a number of steps to confirm that the school is reputable. One of the most important steps is making sure the school is accredited. Teens can find out whether a school is accredited by googling it. School guidance counselors can also help. Accreditation shows that a school has met educational and industry standards of quality. Accredited schools usually have a good reputation, and most employers feel confident about hiring graduates from accredited schools. Moreover, students at accredited schools are eligible for federal student loans. Schools that are not accredited cannot offer this option.

Other useful steps include talking with alumni and current students about their experiences and getting the opinion of industry professionals. Questioning school officials about licensing, certification, and job placement statistics is helpful too. It is especially important for potential enrollees to carefully read any contracts the school requires them to sign. Individuals should look for information about the program's total cost, the length of the program, and whether there is a refund policy. Interested students should not sign anything that doesn't feel right to them.

Nevertheless, despite possible problems, career-focused education programs remain an excellent path for high school graduates who want to work with their hands and learn through doing. These programs give high school graduates the opportunity to learn marketable skills that offer them an excellent route to a wide range of careers in flourishing industries.

Chapter Four

Joining the Workforce

Mason is a young man who loves cars. Ever since he was a little boy, he has helped at the auto dealership his family owns. Although Mason was a good student, he had no desire to continue his education after high school. He always wanted to join his father and older brother in the family business. He explains, "My dad didn't go to college. My brother didn't go to college. Seeing how successful they are in life, I knew I didn't need to go to college to make a living. I knew it wasn't something I wanted to do. . . . I've been in cars my whole life. . . . There wasn't anything I liked more than this."[20]

Jumping into the Workforce

Mason's family ties gave him an advantage when it came to being hired, but not all recent high school graduates have a family business that they can jump into. Lacking experience, higher education, or career training, they may have problems securing a well-paying job in a field that interests them. Yet many young people choose to enter the labor force immediately after high school.

There are lots of reasons young people choose this path. Some teens are tired of or did not enjoy going to school and would rather work than continue going to school. Some enter the workforce to help their families financially. Others are reluctant to take out college loans, especially if they are unsure about what they want to study. Going straight to work gives these teens time to think about what they really want to do. This was the case for Melody, a teen who decided to join the labor force after graduation. She says, "I thought, gosh dang it, I don't know anything about myself or the world. I can't throw myself in debt when I have no idea what I am doing."[21]

But no matter the reason, deciding to go to work immediately after graduating from high school has both benefits and drawbacks. One benefit is that joining the workforce helps young people to become more self-sufficient. Earning a salary is a first step in learning to manage and budget money, which is a vital life skill. Young workers also get a head start in developing job-seeking skills. Many of their peers will not develop these skills until they graduate from college or vocational school.

However, during economic downturns, individuals who lack experience, higher education, or vocational training may have more trouble landing a job than those with degrees, certificates, or career training. Plus, many careers require a degree or some type of training or certification, which limits a high school grad's employment options. Although it is possible for people with just a high school education to snag a good job, many teens wind up in low-paying, dead-end positions. These types of jobs do not usually provide employee benefits, opportunities for advancement, or job security.

Types of Work

Despite such stumbling blocks, there are occupations that welcome high school graduates, pay living wages, provide generous employee benefits, and offer opportunities for advancement. Some of these jobs can be found in the public sector. Federal, state, and local government agencies employ high school graduates as clerical workers, police and correction officers, firefighters, teacher's aides, library assistants, and transportation workers, among other occupations. The US Postal Service is one of the largest governmental employers of high school graduates. More than 500,000 individuals are employed by the postal service in jobs as mail carriers, postal service clerks, mail sorters, and processing machine operators. Many of these individuals do not have college degrees or postsecondary training, yet they are well compensated for their labor. According to Postal Work, a website that provides information about jobs in the US Postal system, postal workers earn an average annual salary of $52,290. That sum does not include employee benefits, which, when added in, raise the total average compensation to $83,000 or more. These benefits include paid sick leave and vacations; health, life, and dental insurance; and retirement benefits.

These extensive benefits, however, are not limited to postal workers. Most federal, state, and local government employees receive similar perks. To snag a government position, applicants may

A US Postal Service mail carrier delivers mail in Summerfield, Florida. The USPS employs more than 500,000 people, many of whom do not have college degrees.

Starting a Small Business

Rather than working for others, some young people dream of starting their own businesses. Being a small business owner has many advantages. Business owners are their own bosses. They set their own hours, salaries, and company rules. They are also responsible for making business decisions. However, starting a new business is not easy. It takes a strong commitment of time and money to get a new business off the ground. And many new businesses fail. Nevertheless, individuals with innovative ideas and/or in-demand interests and skills often do succeed.

Successful businesses fill a need. Successful small business owners use and market their personal skills and talents to fill that need. For example, someone who loves and is good at caring for animals might consider starting a pet-sitting or dog-walking service in an area that lacks this service. Before starting the business, entrepreneurs are advised to first develop a business plan that describes the business—its finances, goals, and target audience; and its strategy for how to achieve these goals. Once the business is open, the owner can grow the business through networking, advertising, and word of mouth.

have to pass a criminal background check, a written or physical exam, and a drug test before being hired. Interested teens can find lists of openings on job board websites as well as at usajobs.gov, an official website of the federal government.

Large corporations also offer high school graduates great employee benefits. For example, some of the biggest private employers in the United States cover the cost of tuition, books, and fees for employees who want to earn an associate's or bachelor's degree or want to learn new skills that qualify them for certificates and licenses. The corporations team up with colleges and training programs throughout the United States to offer online and in-person classes that cater to and support working people. Amazon, Boeing, Disney, Starbucks, Target, T-Mobile, Verizon, and Walmart are just some of the corporations that offer this benefit.

These programs help businesses attract and retain the best workers, and they strengthen young workers' skills, which enables them to move up the corporate ladder. Lorraine Stomski, Walmart's senior vice president of learning and leadership, explains, "We are creating a path of opportunity for our associates to grow their careers at Walmart, so they can continue to build better lives for themselves and their families. This investment is another way we can support our associates to pursue their passion and purpose while removing the barriers that too often keep adult working learners from obtaining degrees."[22]

Eligibility for these programs differs depending on the employer. Disney, for example, requires individuals to be employed with the company for ninety days before they can take advantage of the program. In contrast, Target employees are eligible for tuition coverage on their first day of employment. Moreover, some companies restrict the fields of study to areas that meet the business' current and future labor needs. Walmart, for instance, pays for certification and degree options in business administration, supply chain management, and cybersecurity, and Boeing gives precedence to individuals who focus their studies on subjects related to science, technology, engineering, and mathematics.

On-the-Job Training

Other companies take on high school graduates as apprentices and interns. Apprenticeships and internships are forms of on-the-job training. Apprentices and interns work beside qualified professionals to hone the skills they need to do a particular job. Usually, internships are completed in a few months, whereas apprenticeships are more extensive and can take up to five years to complete. Most apprenticeships combine work and tuition-free classroom training. Where applicable, they prepare individuals to obtain nationally recognized industry credentials.

Most internships are unpaid, but apprenticeships are paid positions. Although apprentices earn less than skilled professionals, their wages rise progressively as their skills increase. According to the US Department of Labor, 90 percent of apprenticeship graduates can expect to earn an average of $70,000 a year.

Apprenticeships are often associated with blue-collar careers in construction and manufacturing, and internships are generally associated with white-collar occupations. However, in recent years diverse industries have started offering apprenticeship programs. To develop and prepare their future workforce, the health care, financial services, telecommunications, transportation, cybersecurity, engineering, and IT industries all offer apprenticeship programs. John Kinney, executive vice president at the Hartford Financial Services Group, explains, "Our apprenticeship program supports a top priority for The Hartford by helping attract and develop diverse talent outside of the traditional college track, for critical customer-facing roles. Participating students gain tuition support and a full-time position with a leading U.S. insurer, where they can grow their career. . . . It's a win for them and a win for us."[23]

Apprentices and interns work alongside experienced professionals to learn a trade, such as carpentry.

Apprenticeship opportunities are offered through businesses, labor unions, and workforce training programs. Teens can find information about and lists of apprenticeship programs at Apprenticeship.gov. State labor departments and government-sponsored American Job Centers are other good sources of information.

Getting and Keeping a Job

Before high school graduates can start working at any job, whether as an apprentice or a regular employee, they must get hired. However, finding a satisfying job is not always easy. To help in their quest, job seekers can check local bulletin boards, want ads, and online job boards such as Monster.com and ZipRecruiter. Alerting family members, friends, and acquaintances about their job search can also be helpful.

Once individuals have pinpointed promising positions, the next step is submitting a job application and a résumé. Résumés should include the applicant's personal information, education history, paid work and volunteer experiences, skills, and references. Tailoring a résumé to a job's description is a good practice. For example, a résumé for a position at a computer repair business should highlight the applicant's tech skills. If an employer is interested in an applicant, the employer will schedule an interview. Dressing appropriately for the interview, speaking confidently and clearly, and being knowledgeable about the company can help candidates make a good impression.

Once they are hired, young people can take other steps to help them keep their job and, possibly, be promoted. Some of these steps are quite simple and include being prompt, reliable, and courteous. It is also essential to comply with the company's rules and dress code. And, even if the position is not one's dream job, employees are advised to do their best. Recent high school graduates can expect to start at the bottom, but they can work their way up. In fact, when workers give their best efforts, they are more likely to advance in their careers.

Military Branches

There are six branches of the US military: the army, navy, coast guard, marine corps, air force, and space force. Each branch has its own specialty areas.

The army is the oldest and largest branch of the military. It traditionally operates on land. The army offers training in 150 career fields, many of which translate into civilian careers. Many naval careers also translate into civilian life. The navy protects the United States at sea. Naval personnel work on ships, submarines, and aircraft carriers, as well as on land. Coast guard members also serve at sea. They protect US ports and coastal and inland waters. Coast guard members are rarely deployed to foreign combat zones. In contrast, the marine corps is usually the first force to be deployed. Marines operate at sea, on land, and as air support for ground forces. The air force is the chief protector of US airways. Air force personnel fly and maintain different types of aircraft and related equipment. The space force also focuses on the air. This newest military branch is responsible for protecting US interests in space. Individuals interested in aerospace and engineering may be drawn to the space force.

Joining the Military

Joining the military is another path some high school graduates take. The US military is always hiring. Enlisting in the military provides young adults with a job and a guaranteed paycheck. And there are positions for young people with all types of interests because the military offers more than two thousand military occupation specialties. Potential recruits are administered a vocational aptitude test to determine where their skills lie. Based on the results, they are placed in an occupation that is suited to their interests and abilities. Troops are given extensive, ongoing training and educational opportunities to ensure they succeed in their jobs. Since almost every civilian career has a military counterpart, the training, education, and experience service members receive can translate into civilian jobs in related fields.

Service members also receive paid college tuition, a housing allowance or free housing on base, meals, health and dental care, and thirty paid annual vacation days. Moreover, they have opportunities to travel and live abroad and a chance to serve their country. Plus, military veterans qualify for support programs such as small business and home loans, paid college tuition, and free health care.

Novice airmen are sworn into service during a US Air Force basic training graduation in San Antonio, Texas.

Nevertheless, there are drawbacks. Military life does not suit every personality. Troops have limited control over their daily lives. They cannot choose where they are stationed, how they dress or wear their hair, or even control when they can sleep or rest. They must be disciplined and able to follow orders. Moreover, service members face danger as part of their job. They can be deployed to war zones where they may be wounded or killed or where they may have to harm others.

It is important that potential service members are aware of these requirements because enlisting is a huge commitment. Service members sign a binding contract in which they vow to serve for a set length of time. Military personnel must fulfill their terms of service or face serious legal consequences. The length of commitment varies, depending on the branch of the military. The air force, coast guard, and marine corps require a minimum of four years of active duty, whereas the army and navy require at least two years.

Even with these duties and demands, many people thrive in the military. Writer and army sergeant Jordan Mendiola is in this group. Unsure about what he wanted to do after high school, he enlisted right after graduation. "I've made a lot of interesting decisions in my life, but the one that changed my life for the better was joining the army after high school," he says. "It was the mental reset I needed after high school in order to start a new journey. There's nothing I would change about my decision."[24] Indeed, although recent high school graduates who opt to enter the military or the civilian workforce face many challenges, many are glad they did.

> "I've made a lot of interesting decisions in my life, but the one that changed my life for the better was joining the army after high school. . . . It was the mental reset I needed after high school in order to start a new journey."[24]
>
> —Jordan Mendiola, writer and army sergeant

Chapter Five

Taking a Gap Year

Mary is a student at Colorado State University. When she graduated from high school, she thought she might want to go to college eventually but not right away. So, instead of following a more traditional path, she spent the year traveling and studying in China. During this time, which is known as a gap year, she explored Chinese history, politics, and culture, learned Mandarin, and interacted with all sorts of people. Her experience, she says, allowed her to reflect upon her future and grow as a person. She explains, "Taking a gap year was valuable for many reasons. . . . My time abroad helped me decide on a major because I absolutely knew that I wanted to continue learning about cultures, political systems, and languages. . . . I also matured significantly that year by learning how to be an independent adult."[25]

What Is a Gap Year?

Like Mary, many teens choose to take a gap year. A gap year is a break that students take between high school and college or other higher education. Individuals take a gap year for a variety of reasons. Doing so allows young people a chance to decompress before pursuing further formal education, and it gives those who are undecided about their future a chance to explore their interests and passions while learning more about themselves. In the process, participants have an opportunity to immerse themselves in other cultures, learn a language, help the less fortunate, or pursue a lifelong dream, among other options.

What young people do during a gap year varies as much as their reasons for taking one. Traveling, studying and working abroad, volunteering, or pursuing independent projects are all common gap year activities. For example, Matt Marchione, the founder of Ultraviolet Ventures, an investment group, spent his gap year learning more about one of his passions: investing. "During my gap year," he recalls, "I read 75 books, took 21 online courses, . . . [and] went to conferences and summits as the youngest in the room."[26]

Marchione planned his own gap year activities, but some individuals take part in established gap year programs that are offered by groups that specialize in student travel, volunteering, and education. These programs can be expensive, especially if they offer an international travel component. Yet because these programs are structured, they provide participants with a sound way to use their time, which helps participants to get the most out of their experiences.

Taking Time to Travel

Many young people dream of exploring the world, and traveling is a popular gap year activity. Some teens plan their trip on their own and travel independently. Others take part in organized travel programs, which set up participants' itineraries, housing, daily schedules, visas, and transportation. Some combine the two possibilities. Jessie Garson, for instance, is a young woman who spent three months of her gap year hiking in the Himalayas as part of a group travel and leadership program and five months traveling solo through Southeast Asia. She says that both experiences helped her to become more self-reliant, confident, and culturally aware.

Deciding where to go and for how long is a first step in planning gap year travel. International travel is especially popular. However, it can be costly. To make it possible for young people to explore the world, many countries offer them discounts, which can greatly reduce the cost of traveling. Travelers in Europe who are younger than twenty-five are eligible for a 35 percent discount on second-class Eurail tickets. Australia and Japan offer similar rail discounts to students. Young travelers can also save money by staying in low-cost accommodations such as youth hostels rather than pricey hotels. Youth hostels are typically clean and safe. Plus, they are good places to meet other travelers.

Staying in college dorm rooms is another money-saving option that is quite popular in Europe. Websites such as UniversityRooms.com help connect travelers with available rooms. Living with a host family is another affordable possibility, and home-cooked meals are often included in the price. Furthermore, rooming with a local family is a good way to experience local life. Student travel, volunteer, and education programs can connect travelers with host families.

Gap Year Concerns

Taking a gap year has long been a common activity for European and Australian teens, and it has become increasingly popular in the United States in recent years. In fact, many employers and graduate schools look favorably on applicants who have experienced gap year activities such as traveling, volunteering, and learning a new language.

Nevertheless, many young people reject the idea of taking a gap year for fear of jeopardizing their college career. To accommodate newly admitted students who want to participate in a gap year, most colleges allow students to defer their enrollment for a year. However, depending on the college, students who defer their enrollment may lose their scholarships or financial aid. Upon returning to college, students who took a gap year are advised to resubmit the FAFSA to remain eligible.

Traveling is a popular gap year activity. Some gap year participants travel internationally, like these students, who traveled to Paris, France.

Another way gap year travelers save money is by journeying closer to home. Traveling within the United States, in their home state, or in a neighboring state can save young people the cost of airfare while still providing them with the fun and benefits of travel. Virtual travel is another possibility for gap year participants who, due to finances, work, health, or any number of other reasons, are unable to travel in the traditional way.

Learning New Skills

Many gap year travelers use all or some of their time abroad to study subjects that interest them. Learning a new language is especially popular. This is not surprising because being multilingual gives individuals a better understanding of other cultures as well as the ability to communicate with different groups, both of which are highly marketable skills. Mary, who spent part of a gap year learning Mandarin in China, insists, "Learning a language never hurts your chances of getting into a school or landing a job, ever!"[27]

Many gap year programs offer a language-learning component, which is often combined with travel within the host country, and other study options. Participants may take classes at a local university, and some live with local families, where they are immersed in the new language. Sam Feldstein, an Atlanta teen who participated in this type of gap year program in Israel, describes his experience:

> I . . . spend most days at The Hebrew University of Jerusalem on Mount Scopus. There, I broaden my knowledge of many fields in which I have always been interested and establish context for daily life here in Israel. I am taking four classes: Advanced Hebrew, Colloquial Arabic, The Battle over the three Bibles (Jewish Bible, Christian Old Testament, and Muslim Quran), and Technology and Entrepreneurship in Israel. . . . I constantly look forward to applying all that I have learned into my own life. For example, after learning how to read, speak and write Arabic letters, I have been able to read every Arabic street sign. Also, after learning the basics of a conversation in colloquial Arabic, I have gone up and talked to Arabic speakers in their native tongue. . . .
>
> Communicating with people from other religions and cultures heightens my interest in other people from around the world. . . . I have been able to engage in productive communication just in Hebrew, in which I have become nearly fluent in just three months.[28]

Learning a new language is not limited to gap year program enrollees. Independent travelers can enroll in formal language classes abroad. They can also learn a new language by spending their gap year living and traveling in a part of the world where that language is spoken. However, it is not necessary for gap year participants to travel to become multilingual. Young people can learn a new language by using language software or by taking online or local classes.

A new language is not the only thing that teens can gain knowledge of during a gap year. There are gap year programs for creative individuals that combine travel to world art and theater centers with hands-on experiences, classes, and workshops that help develop art, filmmaking, performing, writing, and photography skills. Young adventurers can enroll in less traditional programs too. They can spend up to three months at sea getting instruction in oceanography, marine biology, seamanship, and marine radio operations. Other programs offer participants instruction in scuba diving, sailing, skiing, snowboarding, wilderness survival, and other outdoor activities, which may qualify individuals to become certified instructors in these fields. And to make these experiences available to as many young people as possible, some programs offer scholarships and financial aid.

Many gap year travelers choose to study local languages during their time abroad, like these students, who are in a German language school. Becoming multilingual has many personal and professional benefits.

Volunteering

Volunteering is another popular component of many teens' gap year activities. Lots of gap year participants combine volunteering with travel. Gap year volunteers serve as a force for positive change all over the world. They work to eliminate illiteracy, end poverty, support wildlife, and protect the environment, among many other causes. As part of their service, they may care for elephants in Thailand, teach English in Bali, or build schools in Fiji. Some rescue sea turtle eggs in Costa Rica, and others tutor and mentor disadvantaged children in South Africa. But no matter the destination or the service activity, most participants say that the experience changed them and their lives for the better. Bethany Dunne, a young Canadian gap year participant who served as a child care volunteer in Tanzania, relates, "Volunteering was truly a life changing experience that I will treasure for the rest of my days. . . . I think I learned more from the kids than I ever could have taught them."[29]

Nonprofit, religion-based, and other structured gap year programs sponsor international volunteer opportunities. Some provide

Travel Safety

Traveling independently gives gap year participants more flexibility and freedom than gap year travel programs offer. However, since participants travel in a group and are often accompanied by an experienced guide, traveling with an organized gap year program is usually safer. Even so, there are measures that independent travelers can take to keep safe.

The FBI provides safety tips for US students traveling abroad on its website. It advises young travelers to take the following precautions:

- Provide their family with their itinerary
- Familiarize themselves with the culture of the countries they visit so that they do not draw unfriendly attention to themselves
- Make copies of their passports, airplane tickets, driver's licenses, and credit cards and keep these separate from the originals
- Never invite strangers into their hotel rooms or get into a car with strangers
- Never carry large amounts of cash or unnecessary credit cards
- Avoid civil disturbances and illegal activities

Staying safe will allow travelers the time to enjoy their surroundings and to engage with the local culture.

volunteers compensation in the form of free room and board or a small stipend. Other programs are fee based. In almost all instances, airfare is not provided.

To avoid the cost of airfare, lots of gap year participants volunteer within their home communities. Some sign up with a national service organization such as AmeriCorps, a federal agency that connects volunteers with more than two thousand organizations throughout the United States that are dedicated to strengthening communities. Volunteers tackle all sorts of projects, including providing disaster relief, maintaining national parks, mentoring children, and writing grant proposals. Individuals can volunteer for anywhere from a few days to years. Volunteers who serve for at least three months receive a financial award, which may help them pay for college in the future. Depending on the project, volunteers may also receive room and board or a small living allowance, health insurance, uniforms, and cardiopulmonary resuscitation training. But the reward is much greater than these perks. Amelia Glickman, a young woman who served as an AmeriCorps literacy tutor in California during her gap year, puts it this way:

> I am incredibly grateful . . . to be able to have an impact on these young children, and to be immersed in a bilingual environment. This full-time volunteer opportunity has given me a job-like experience right out of high school, and I feel much more prepared for the world. Most of all, each day I can just have fun and build relationships with the preschoolers I tutor. It is humbling knowing I am making a difference in their lives.[30]

Pursuing a Dream

Whereas some young people spend a gap year traveling, developing new skills, or volunteering, others use the time to pursue

Many people volunteer for worthy causes during gap years. They might choose activities as diverse as rescuing sea turtles like this one, or mentoring disadvantaged children, or doing environmental work.

a long-held passion or dream, which they hope will lead to a future career. For instance, ever since *Your Teen* magazine manager Eca Taylor's daughter started taking ballet classes as a child, she dreamed of becoming a professional ballerina. Nonetheless, upon the urging of her teachers and family, she applied to colleges. She planned on double majoring in dance and a still-undecided, more practical subject. But when a professional dance company formed in her hometown and offered her a chance to join the company, she decided to defer college to follow her dream. "She had a chance to do what she had always dreamed of doing," Taylor explains. "We didn't want her to have any regrets later. . . . We hope she will go to college one day after this gap year, just not this year. Maybe not even next year. We're okay with that. In the words of a dear friend, she's 'livin' the dream.'"[31]

Whether or not Taylor's daughter's decision to pursue her dream will lead to fame and fortune remains to be seen. But even if it does not, she—like many other teens who spend a gap year trying to become professional artists, bloggers, writers, entertainers, and social media influencers, among other passions—had the chance to follow her dream, which is what life after high school is all about.

Source Notes

Introduction: At a Crossroads

1. Jessica, interview with the author, Las Cruces, New Mexico, October 13, 2022.
2. Jessica, interview.
3. Zakirah White, "Life After High School: 'It's All About Balance,'" *Vox Blog,* Vox ATL, February 13, 2020. www.voxatl.org.

Chapter One: Preparing and Exploring

4. Quoted in Children's Minnesota, "Life After High School." www.child rensmn.org.
5. Quoted in Genevieve Morgan, *Undecided: Navigating Life and Learning After High School*. Minneapolis: Zest, 2020, p. 61.
6. Eric S. Burdon, "10 Ways to Learn About Yourself," Medium, November 17, 2019. www.medium.com.
7. Indeed Editorial Team, "Job Shadowing for High School Students (and Why It Is Important)," Indeed, September 15, 2021. www.indeed.com.

Chapter Two: Going to College

8. Quoted in Team GaryVee, "Life After High School: The Traditional Student," Gary Vee. www.garyvaynerchuk.com.
9. White, "Life After High School."
10. Quoted in Daytripper University, "Students Speak: Why I Chose My College," January 25, 2020. www.daytripperuniversity.com.
11. Quoted in Daytripper University, "Students Speak."
12. Quoted in Daytripper University, "Students Speak."
13. Quoted in Morgan, *Undecided,* p. 121.
14. Morgan, *Undecided,* p. 104.

Chapter Three: Opting for Technical and Vocational Training

15. Quoted in SkillPointe, "How a Random Email Transformed Charlie Tran's Career Plans," August 18, 2021. https://skillpointe.com.

16. Quoted in Aspen Institute, "Partnering with Community Colleges," Skilled Trades Playbook. www.skilledtradesplaybook.org.
17. Quoted in SkillPointe, "'I Had My Best Opportunity in Front of Me the Entire Time,' says HVAC Tech," August 6, 2021. https://skillpointe.com.
18. Quoted in Meghan Gravel, "From CCV Degree to a Job in IT," CCV, December 1, 2021. https://ccv.edu.
19. Quoted in Aveda Institutes, "Great Stories Start at Aveda Institutes: Daniel Holzberger." https://avedafi.edu.

Chapter Four: Joining the Workforce

20. Quoted in Jack Healy, "Out of High School, into Real Life," *New York Times,* June 23, 2017. www.nytimes.com.
21. Quoted in Timothy Snyder, "Why Some People Don't Go to College Right After High School," That College Book, December 19, 2018. https://thatcollegebook.com.
22. Quoted in Walmart, "Walmart to Pay 100% of College Tuition and Books for Associates," July 27, 2021. https://corporate.walmart.com.
23. Quoted in ApprenticeshipUSA, "Earn While You Learn Today," August 2022. www.apprenticeship.gov.
24. Jordan Mendiola, "Joining the Army After High School was a Good Decision," *Illumination* (blog), Medium, January 30, 2021. www.medium.com.

Chapter Five: Taking a Gap Year

25. Mary, "I Took a Gap Year: How It Went and How I Transitioned to College," Colorado State University, January 19, 2021. www.admissions.colostate.edu.
26. Max Marchione, "How I Took the Learning Gap Year That Changed My Life," October 2021. www.maxmarchione.com.
27. Mary, "I Took a Gap Year."
28. Sam Feldstein, "My Gap Year Experience," JumpSpark, November 23, 2021. https://jumpsparkatl.org.
29. Quoted in International Volunteer HQ, "Volunteer in Tanzania." www.volunteerhq.org.
30. Quoted in AmeriCorps, "Amelia Glickman: AmeriCorps Member." www.americorps.gov.
31. Eca Taylor, "My Daughter Is Taking a Gap Year (Try Saying That at a Cocktail Party)," *Your Teen,* October 22, 2015. www.yourteenmag.com.

Organizations and Websites

Apprenticeship.gov
www.apprenticeship.gov
Sponsored by the US government, this website connects businesses, job seekers, and educational institutions with apprenticeship opportunities.

Bureau of Labor Statistics (BLS)
www.bls.gov
The BLS is a government agency that provides all sorts of information related to labor, including an *Occupational Outlook Handbook* that gives data on hundreds of occupations, including salaries, educational requirements, and more.

CareerOneStop
www.careeronestop.org
Sponsored by the US Department of Labor, CareerOneStop provides information on different careers, career training, and vocational training institutions. It also offers an interest assessment tool, job postings, and a scholarship finder, among other resources.

College Board
www.collegeboard.org
The College Board is a nonprofit organization that develops standardized tests. It houses a wealth of information about college planning, admissions, and financial aid as well as information on hundreds of colleges on its website.

Federal Student Aid
www.studentaid.gov
Federal Student Aid is the largest provider of student financial assistance in the United States. As part of the US Department of Education, it manages federal student financial aid programs and provides information and assistance to students applying for and receiving federal financial aid. The FAFSA application can be accessed on this site.

Gap Year Association

www.gapyearassociation.org

This nonprofit organization oversees accreditation for gap year programs. It offers information about taking a gap year as well as gap year activities, programs, and scholarships.

Scholarships.com

www.scholarships.com

Scholarships.com helps students find financial aid. Users can find, be matched with, and apply for scholarships on the website.

For Further Research

Books

Edward B. Fiske, *Fiske Guide to Colleges 2023.* Naperville, IL: Source-books, 2022.

Brian Harris, *After High School: A Guide to Help You Plan Your Future After High School.* 3rd ed. Self-published, CGS Communications, 2020.

Kevin Ray Johnson, *Now What?* Chicago: Joshua Tree, 2020.

Katie Sharp, *College and Career Planning.* San Diego: ReferencePoint, 2021.

Kristin M. White, *The Complete Guide to the Gap Year: The Best Things to Do Between High School and College*. Darien, CT: Nota Bene, 2019.

Internet Sources

Indeed Editorial Team, "11 College Benefits to Weigh When Pursuing Higher Education," December 12, 2019 (updated September 13, 2022). www.indeed.com.

Mila Koumpilova, "In Urban Districts, a New Embrace of Career and Technical Programs," *Washington Post*, August 19, 2022. www.washington post.com.

Teddy Nykiel, Anna Helhoski, and Eliza Haverstock, "How to Pay for College: 8 Expert-Approved Tips," NerdWallet, December 7, 2022. www.nerd wallet.com.

Occupational Information Network, "O*NET Interest Profiler," O*NET Resource Center. www.onetcenter.org.

Pearson Online Academy, "The Ultimate Guide to College Preparation." www.pearsononlineacademy.com.

Technical Education Post, "US Manufacturers Can't Find Enough Skilled Workers to Fill Open Jobs," Tech Ed Magazine, June 6, 2021. www .techedmagazine.com.

Geoff Williams, "25 Best Jobs for High School Graduates," *U.S. News & World Report*, February 28, 2022. https://money.usnews.com.

Index

Picture Credits